GET ACTIVE!

YOGA

Alix Wood

WAYLAND
www.waylandbooks.co.uk

> All sports can be dangerous. Do not attempt any of the skills in this book without supervision from a trained adult expert.

Wayland
First Published in Great Britain in 2019 by Wayland.

Copyright © Hodder & Stoughton

Published by permission of Gareth Stevens Publishing, New York, NY, USA.

HB ISBN: 978 1 5263 1174 0
PB ISBN: 978 1 5263 1175 7

Produced for Wayland by Alix Wood
Art direction and content research: Kevin Wood
Editor: Eloise Macgregor
Editor for Gareth Stevens: Kerri O'Donnell
Consultant: Molly Robertson

Photo credits:
Cover, 1, 3, 4, 5, 6 top, 8, 9, 10, 11, 13, 16, 18 top, 22, 23 top, 27 bottom, 28, 29, 30 © Shutterstock; all other images © Greg Dennis.

Acknowledgments
With grateful thanks to James Latus, Josh Latus, Storm Brennon, Kieron Turk, Will Ferris, Corie Stubbs and Ellena Harrison.

Printed in China

Wayland
An imprint of
Hachette Children's Group
Part of Hodder & Stoughton
Carmelite House
50 Victoria Embankment
London EC4Y 0DZ

An Hachette UK Comany
www.hachette.co.uk
www.hachettechildrens.co.uk

FSC
www.fsc.org

MIX
Paper from
responsible sources
FSC® C104740

CONTENTS

WHY DO YOGA?

Yoga has been practised for thousands of years. It is believed to unite the mind, the body and the spirit. Yoga helps you become more aware of your body's **posture**, **alignment** and movement.

Yoga is a great way to get fit. It makes the body more **flexible** and helps you to relax. Practising yoga can make you happier and feel peaceful, too. Yoga is thought to help improve your memory and concentration. Many schools now start the day with a yoga session to help concentrate their student's minds. Yoga is also believed to help with anxiety and depression, and help lower your blood pressure and your pulse rate.

Yoga is fun and great exercise.

In a yoga class, the students usually place their mats facing the front. Leave a little space around your mat so you have space to do the poses. The students often sit cross-legged waiting for the class to start, or they do some gentle stretches. The teacher may start the class with a breathing exercise or **meditation**. This is followed by warm-up poses, more vigorous poses, then stretches and then final relaxation exercises.

Yoga classes may use blankets to roll up and use as props for some poses. Some classes use blocks and straps (below) as well. The blocks act as props and the straps help in poses where you need to hold your feet, for example, but can't quite reach.

Wear stretchy exercise trousers or shorts. A fitted T-shirt is best. Baggy T-shirts can slide up when you are upside down. You can usually rent yoga mats to start with. Yoga is usually done barefoot.

TRY THIS

Most yoga classes end a session by saying 'namaste', which means 'I bow to you' in Hindi.

MEDITATION

Meditation is an important part of learning yoga. You don't have to learn to meditate to enjoy yoga, but it is generally considered to be part of the experience.

Yoga means union. Meditation is a way for people doing yoga to unite their body and mind. Meditation improves your ability to focus on things, including your yoga. Benefits of meditation include a decrease in blood pressure, improved breathing and a slower resting heart rate. Chemicals in the body that are associated with stress may get lower as well.

You can meditate in any still position. Sitting is the most common posture. A simple cross-legged pose is good for beginners.

Many people like to meditate near the calming presence of water.

To try to meditate, create a peaceful atmosphere and wear comfortable clothing. Concentrate on one thing, such as your breathing, a word or sensations you feel in your body. If your thoughts start to wander, take them back to your object of focus. To prevent other thoughts coming into your mind, try looking at an object such as a candle. Once your mind is clear of thought, you will feel calm, yet aware. People say this feeling cannot be described by words.

This child's pose is physically relaxing and one of the best yoga poses for mental relaxation.

BREATHING

Controlling your breathing is important during yoga. Breathing correctly brings more oxygen to the blood and the brain.

Yoga breathing techniques help increase your lung **capacity**. Just as with meditation, concentrating on your breathing develops your focus, too. It fights away stress and relaxes the body. Breathing correctly during a pose is important. If your breathing isn't relaxed, your body can't relax into the pose. If your body isn't relaxed, your mind can't relax. And if your mind isn't relaxed, you can't draw the full benefits from your yoga.

Yoga breathing control is called pranayama. The breath sets the rhythm for the practice. When you **inhale**, move into pose. When you **exhale**, move out of it. Your movements should match your breath.

The following yoga breathing exercises can make you feel dizzy, so make sure you're with a trained adult when you try out these techniques. Kapalabhati is a cleaning breath. Breaths are short, rapid and strong. The lungs work as a pump, creating pressure as they expel the air and remove waste from the air passages.

Take two normal breaths. Breathe in.

Breathe out, pulling in your **abdomen**. Repeat twenty times, emphasising breathing out. Finally, breathe in fully and hold your breath for as long as you can. Slowly breathe out.

TRY THIS

Alternate nostril breathing helps some people to settle the mind and the body. Only try this under the supervision of a trained expert.

Hold your hand as shown in the picture. Inhale through your left nostril, closing the right with your thumb. Count to four. Hold your breath, closing both nostrils. Count to sixteen. Exhale through the right nostril, closing the left with the ring and little fingers. Count to eight. Inhale using the right nostril, keeping the left nostril closed with the ring and little fingers. Count to four. Hold your breath, closing both nostrils, and count to sixteen. Exhale using the left nostril, keeping the right closed with the thumb. Count to eight.

Relaxing Breathing

You can help get rid of stress using these yogic breathing techniques.

Sit comfortably in a chair. Close your eyes and picture a swan gliding peacefully across a crystal-clear lake. Now, like the swan, let your breath flow along in a long, smooth, peaceful movement. Inhale and exhale through your nose. If your nose is blocked, use your nose and mouth, or just your mouth. Inhale and exhale as deeply as you can, and repeat this 20 times. Then, gradually let your breath return to normal. Take a few moments to sit with your eyes closed and notice how different you feel overall.

BREATHING

Yogic breathing — dos and don'ts

- if you have problems with your lungs, such as a cold or asthma, or if you have heart disease, ask your doctor before trying breathing techniques
- don't practise breathing exercises when the air is too cold or too hot
- avoid practicing in polluted air, including the smoke from **incense**. Practise breath control outdoors or with an open window
- don't strain your breathing. Remain relaxed while doing breathing exercises

One method of breathing used in yoga is called ujjayi breathing. The breathing is quite noisy, which helps focus your attention on each breath. The breath is done through the nose. First fill your lower abdomen, then your lower rib cage and finally your upper chest and throat. As the throat passage is narrowed the passage of air creates a 'rushing' sound.

Ujjayi breathing should sound like the ocean. The 'ocean sound' is created by moving the **glottis** as the air passes in and out.

SEATED EXERCISES

Yoga isn't all about tying yourself in complicated knots. There are some simpler seated poses that are very good at improving your strength and flexibility.

This seated twist pose stretches your shoulders, hips and back. It helps increase circulation and tones the abdomen. If you find this too hard, make it easier by keeping your bottom leg straight and place both hands on your raised knee. If your lower back rounds forwards sit on a folded blanket.

Seated twist

- Sit on the floor with your legs extended.
- Cross your right foot over the outside of your left thigh. Bend your left knee. Keep your right knee pointed toward the ceiling.
- Place your left elbow to the outside of your right knee and your right hand on the floor behind you.
- Twist right as far as you can, moving from your abdomen. Keep both sides of your bottom on the floor. Stay for one minute.
- Switch sides and repeat.

This boat pose is great at exercising your stomach muscles and helps your balance.

Boat pose

Sit with your legs out in front of you. Lean back and bend your knees, lifting your legs off the floor. Lean back further. Hold your thighs with your hands and pull in your lower back. Stretch your arms to the front, with your palms facing your body. After 5 to 10 breaths, slowly straighten your legs. Your feet should be higher than your head. Hold the pose for 5 to 10 breaths, then slowly release.

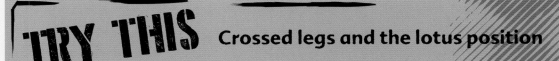

TRY THIS   Crossed legs and the lotus position

1

A cross-legged position is a good way to meditate, and is a good way to sit in between poses in class.

2

To do a lotus, start cross-legged. Place one foot on the thigh, sole upwards. Slowly try to lift the other foot and place it on the other thigh.

STANDING POSES

Standing poses help open up your chest and shoulders and help you build long, lean, strong arms and legs.

Doing a tree pose helps you with your balance and focus. Try it on both legs.

1. Stand with your arms at your sides.

2. Shift your weight onto your right leg and place the sole of your left foot inside your right thigh, keeping your hips facing forwards.

3. Once balanced, bring your hands in front of you in a prayer position, with your palms together.

4. On an inhalation, extend your arms over your shoulders, palms separated and facing each other. Stay for 30 seconds.

5. Repeat the pose using the other leg.

The warrior pose is great for leg strength. It's important to keep your body straight over your hips.

① Start by doing a low lunge, with your feet far apart. Bend your front knee.

② Roll your back heel to the ground. Drop your shoulders and turn them parallel to your mat.

③ Reach your arms out, palms down, parallel to the ground. Keep your body vertical over your hips, with your front knee directly over your ankle.

Gaze out over your right hand. Hold the pose for one minute. Then try doing it on the other side.

Warrior and Triangle

Yoga doesn't just involve separate poses. Part of the workout you get is from moving from one pose to another.

There are several different warrior poses. You can try moving through them all. The pose on the right is called warrior I. Remember to inhale as you move into a pose, and exhale as you move out of it.

TRY THIS

Try this variation of warrior pose, warrior III.

Start from warrior pose, then hold both arms up, palms together. Lean forwards and exhale. Lift your back foot and straighten your leg.

The triangle pose will help expand your shoulders and chest. This pose increases flexibility in your hip and neck joints. It also stretches the muscles in your spine, your **calves** and your thighs.

Start from a warrior position.

Straighten your front leg, and follow your front hand forwards, down to your shin or the floor.

Reach your top arm straight up, and bring your body and legs in the same line.

ARM BALANCES

This pose is called the downward dog. It is usually one of the first poses you will learn in a yoga class.

Downward dog uses the strength of your arms and legs to evenly stretch your spine. It stretches your hips, **hamstrings** and calves. It opens your chest and shoulders and tones your arms and abdomen. It even tones your hands and feet, preparing you for standing poses and arm balances.

Start on your hands and knees, with your shoulders over your wrists and your toes tucked.

Make a tall 'V' shape by lifting your hips straight up, sinking upper chest and shoulders, and relaxing down the backs of your legs into your heels.

The plank builds arm and abdomen strength. You might find your arms shaking as you practise it at first.

The plank
Start on your hands and knees, shoulders directly over your wrists.

Tuck your toes, extend your legs, and walk your feet back until your shoulders, hips and ankles form a straight line.

TRY THIS

Stop your plank from sagging by inhaling to pull your abdomen in and straighten your lower back.

The sideways plank
From a plank, lift your hips up and shift your weight onto one hand. Roll your whole body to that side. Your shoulders, hips and ankles should be in one straight line. Reach your top arm straight up.

The Crow

The crow builds strength in your arms, inner thighs and abdomen. It looks really cool, too!

The crow posture can be painful for the wrists at first. To make it easier, try shifting your weight forwards until you feel some pressure on your wrists, and then practise lifting one foot and then the other off the ground until your wrists build up strength to lift both feet off the ground together.

1 Squat with your feet apart. Put your palms on the ground under your shoulders. Bend your arms slightly, and squeeze your knees firmly around your elbows or upper arms.

2 Rock your weight forwards into your hands, coming up high on your toes. Lift your feet off the ground.

3

Your feet will lift easily off the ground when your weight is more in front of your hands than behind them. Lean your shoulders out past your wrists to shift your weight forwards.

Try doing a half crow if you find the crow too difficult.

From a downward dog, lift one leg and bend your knee, pressing your calf into the back of your thigh. Roll your shoulders forwards over your wrists and bring your knee to the outside of your upper arm. Bend your elbows slightly and shift your shoulders forwards to bring your back foot off the ground.

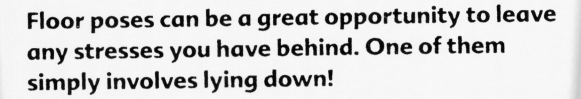

FLOOR POSES

Floor poses can be a great opportunity to leave any stresses you have behind. One of them simply involves lying down!

It's called the corpse pose for a reason. It gives your body and mind a rest, surrendering and letting go of control. The corpse pose relaxes your central nervous system and calms your mind.

The corpse pose

Lie on your back with your knees bent. Lift your hips off the floor and lengthen your spine along the floor. Then drop your hips down again. Straighten your legs and let your feet fall out naturally to the sides. Slide your shoulders away from your ears and tuck your shoulder blades under you. Stretch out your arms and rest them loosely away from your body.

Let your head feel heavy. Breathe naturally in and out through the nose. Fill your throat, chest and abdomen with every inhale. Exhale fully. Relax your eyes and focus on the inside of your forehead between your eyebrows. Feel a sense of stillness and calm. Stay for 5 to 30 minutes.

In child's pose you can hold your arms out to the front, like this, or drape them alongside your legs.

TRY THIS

Meditate!

The child's pose is not only physically relaxing. It's mentally relaxing, too. Try meditating in child pose.

The child's pose

Kneel on the floor, knees slightly apart and big toes touching. Lean forwards until your forehead touches the floor. Let your face, neck and shoulders relax. Breathe deeply into the abdomen. Release all tension away from the body as you sink deeper into the pose with each breath. Let your arms drape along your sides, palms up, or place them palms down in front of you.

The pigeon

Begin in a push-up position, with your palms under your shoulders. Place your right knee on the floor near your shoulder with your right heel by your left hip. Lower down to your forearms. Bring your left leg down with the top of your foot on the floor. Stay on your forearms, or, if you're more flexible, lower to floor and extend your arms in front of you, like in this picture.

Cobras and Bridges

Both of these poses exercise your spine and chest. The bridge strengthens your legs. The cobra is great for building arm strength, too.

The cobra
Lie face down on the floor with your hands just in front of your shoulders. Your legs should be extended with the tops of your feet on the floor. Push strongly down with your pelvis and push up using your thumbs and index fingers. Raise your chest. Feel the power and stretch in your lower back.

TRY THIS
Is it a cobra or an upward facing dog?

These two yoga poses look identical. The difference is where the power is coming from. In upward facing dog, the strength is in the shoulders and the rest of body falls away. In cobra, the power is in the lower back; the arms are merely props.

To do a king cobra, try to raise your legs to touch your head.

The bridge is called Chatush Padasana, which means 'four foot pose'. Your weight should be distributed evenly between your feet and shoulders, as if you had four feet.

1 Lie flat on your back. Bend your knees straight up, bringing your heels just behind your hips. Exhale and lift your hips up to knee height.

2 Grasp your ankles or **interlace** your fingers with your arms straight. Squeeze your shoulder blades together.

TRY THIS

If you find a bridge difficult, try using straps and blocks to help you achieve this pose.

THE HARD STUFF

Although the main mission of yoga is balance, it can seriously challenge your strength and flexibility, too.

Headstands can be very challenging. They require great core strength and courage. Headstands are great for focus and calming the mind. Muscular bodies can find headstands hard. Some very fit people have tight hamstrings, shoulders and backs.

1. Make sure the space around you is safe if you fall. Get on your hands and knees.

2. Lower your forearms to the ground. Position your elbows under your shoulders.

3. Clasp your fingers together behind your head. Put the top of your head on the ground.

4. Walk your feet towards you until your hips are over your head. Lift one leg, then the other until both are straight up in the air.

Getting up is the tricky part. Try just lifting one leg at first and bending your knee so your calf is touching your thigh.